ABINGTON COMMUNITY LIBRARY
CLARKS SUMMIT, PA.

S0-DNL-114

The
Life of

Mac

Cover and interior design by Lee Sebastiani & Lori Sebastiani,

Copyright © 2012 by Francis X. McDonnell. All rights reserved.

9781936936038
1st printing September 2012
Printed in the United States of America

The Life of Mac

A Memoir

FRANCIS X.
McDONNELL

Editor's Note

I asked Mac why he wanted to write a memoir.

"For the last couple of years, I've been getting older, and I've had cancer, a new hip, a pacemaker....But at 90 I'm still going strong. Everybody tells me that I've had an interesting life, and I wanted to remind my kids about some of the things I've done. So I decided to write a book. I'm proud that I was able to help so many people in my life, and I'm glad I'm still able to help them."

And that's Mac. As I worked with Mac to assemble his handwritten drafts, newspaper clippings, letters, documents, interviews, programs and photos, I realized that the theme of this book, and of Mac's whole life, truly is *helping others*. It is reflected in his long career in employment service, in his Bronze Star (awarded for saving lives, not taking them), and in the gratitude of countless individuals for his generosity and advocacy, not to mention his homemade jellies.

I'd like to thank Mac's family and *Scranton Times* reporter Josh McAuliffe for their valuable assistance. A special thank-you to Mac's granddaughter Clare Stevens, who conducted a superb interview with Mac for the Story Corps program.

—Lee Sebastiani

FOREWORD

If you look for one word to define Mac, it is the one word "unselfish." Almost everyone who has come in contact with him knows the tremendous distance that Mac will go to for anyone in need. His middle name should have been "unselfish," because that is what he is—to the veterans of Vietnam, to the young veterans of Iraq and Afghanistan —for veterans of all ages, there is nothing he will not try to make their lives happier.

He is always doing something for his community. At 90 years of age to be raising money for the local library in Peckville so others can benefit! This is Mac in action. He is always there no matter who calls—for those seeking a job, for those looking for a better life, for these in need and want—Mac is always there.

His family knows his unselfishness. His community knows his unselfishness.

His Church also knows his unselfishness. We have been blessed to have a person of this generosity of spirit and when you think of it, he should have been given the middle name "unselfish" when he was given the sacrament of confirmation. It applies to him in every way.

Father Mark Connolly

ABOUT Francis McDonnell

In January of 1961 when President John F. Kennedy urged Americans to ask themselves what they could do to help their country, attracting bright, energetic, and accomplished citizens to a career in public service was deemed vital to the success of the nation.

In Pennsylvania, the men and women who had witnessed and weathered World War 2 were challenged to continue to strengthen their communities and commonwealth. Countless individuals answered President Kennedy's call. It was a moment I remembered when entering public life years later.

But nearly a generation before, there was a man who had gone from serving his country in war to serving it in peace. When Kennedy spoke, this man was already a veteran of a hard fought war and a public employee with a career of over 15 years already behind him. He knew the importance of public service, the help that government can provide, and that he had the skills to be very good at his job.

Few men, few Americans, have served his fellow citizens better, longer, or with more distinction than Francis X. McDonnell.

It has been my pleasure to know Frank throughout my years of work in the state legislature. Frank was an active state employee and continues to be a forceful presence in local politics and charitable works. We who have worked with Frank and have seen his energetic and effective efforts on behalf of good people and good causes know him to be champion of the needy. His big heart has produced big results, whether it was his work on behalf of the unemployed and the over-looked or the generous gift of his time and talent in numerous successful local projects. Frank got things done, and he still does.

Frank's work on behalf of veterans exemplifies this spirit. Because of his selfless efforts, men like Medal of Honor recipient Gino Merli will never be forgotten, nor will the sacrifice of other local servicemen and women. He is a leader in preserving memories, offering first-hand testimony on patriotism, honor, and devotion to our nation.

To see Frank McDonnell work is to be given a view of just how much one man, gifted with a strong personality and character, can motivate and energize others. Over and over, Frank has taken on projects, whether from their start or stalled, and interjected his leadership and know-how. Many of those countless endeavors met success due only to Frank's contributions. Frank has been at the center of so many of the good works done in our area that his place in the hearts of all of who joined him in those efforts is unrivaled.

For me, to work and know Frank these many years has been a distinct honor. Men and women of Frank's age are now labeled by a grateful nation as a part of the Greatest Generation. For us who know, respect, and revere him, Francis X. McDonnell is all of that for sure, but much more. He, like no other, personifies the very best attributes of the admirable life-long vocation of public servant.

WITH warm Regards
Rep. E.G. Staback

Pennsylvania State Representative
Edward G. Staback

DEDICATION

I consider myself the luckiest person in the world. This book is dedicated to my beloved family—my sister Margaret; my brother Edward; my children Ellen, Erin, Marty and Elizabeth. And of course their mother Isobel. I miss her very much.

I also dedicate *The Life of Mac* to :

- a REALLY SPECIAL FRIEND. I've known Father Mark Connolly since around 1960, and he's still a most loyal friend
- Father Joe Kopacz, former pastor at St. James and still a close friend
- Father Blake, past pastor at St. James and Father Gerard, current pastor at Queen of Angels.

To the medical team who *keep me moving*:

Dr. Majernick—family doctor

Dr. John Lundin—heart attack, stroke, pacemaker

Dr. John Doherty—orthopedic surgery (hip, both knees)

Dr. Jay Bannon—cancer surgery (2005)

Dr. James Stefanelli—neurologist

Dr. Joseph Chun—orthopedic surgeon

Dr. Joseph Gershoy—podiatrist

Dr. Anthony DeCarli—dentist

Dr. Cynthia Charnetski—ophthalmologist

Dr. Linda Thomas—cancer (June 30, 2011)

Dr. Christian Adonizio—cancer surgery (2005 and 2011)

And finally, to some *special friends*:

Carolyn Drury (companion for eight years), Margaret Olsewski, Ray Ceccotti, Sr., Bob Mellow, and Fred Lettieri.

I was three or four years of age. The bathtub at the upper right was placed in the kitchen.

FAMILY AND YOUTH

I was born in a house on Number Five Hill in the town of Archbald, Pennsylvania on the seventh of January, 1922, to Patrick McDonnell and Alta Otto.

My father was the son of an Irish immigrant and my mother was the daughter of a German immigrant. I had three brothers—Tom, Mark and Edward—and two sisters, Margaret and Mary Lou.

The average life expectancy in 1922 was 54 years. My dad's parents died when he was eleven years old. He started working in the coal mines to support his brothers and sisters, Big Tom, Mark, Helen, and Katherine. My dad's sister Rose was sent to Exeter to live with a cousin, and sister Molly went to Scranton to live with Uncle Bill and Aunt Nell.

Great Aunt Rose Price moved in with the family and acted as both mother and father. Rose McDonnell was certified as a schoolteacher after two years of advanced study at East Stroudsburg State College. My Aunt Helen went to King's County Hospital in New York and became a registered nurse. Uncle Mark was an auto mechanic. Aunt Molly earned a business degree.

My brother Tom became an electrical engineer. My brother Mark attended the University of Scranton under a football scholarship; my brother Edward finished college in

Philadelphia. Sister Margaret too became a registered nurse. My mom and dad raised Mary Lou, who was developmentally disabled, until her death. Then she lived with Mark and Mary and their family in Binghamton, New York.

I grew up on Dutch Hill. It was great. We were all poor; we thought that was the way it was supposed to be. We played many games like Johnny Ride the Pony, Catnip, softball, baseball, and Catnip. To play Catnip, we used to take a broom and cut it off in pieces. We'd sharpen both ends and hit one end to make the piece fly up in the air to outscore the other team. Twenty one was out.

I had a lot of good friend, had a lot of fun, playing games together. We were all in the same category, we had nothing. We were on welfare a lot of the time. My father worked at the WPA projects, when the mines weren't open.

My parents were terrific. They raised six children. During the Depression things were pretty tough. Because of World War II and the Depression, all six kids and mom and dad never sat down at the same table once. Even for my mom and dad's fiftieth anniversary, we could never get the family together because of unemployment, wars, and everything else. The family was scattered all over the United States.

We never grew up together. There was a difference of twenty years

between me and my youngest sister, Mary Lou. And I might even mention here something interesting, comparing it to today. I was working at the Picatinny Arsenal in New jersey in 1941. In those days we were very innocent, about everything in life I guess, and I came home one weekend and I asked my dad, "Where's Mom?"

Mac is in white.

He said, "You have a new baby sister. She's down at the Mid-Valley Hospital." I didn't even know my mother was pregnant.

Well, my father was from an Irish family and they were good people. All his brothers lived close by in the neighborhood. The same thing about my mom. We had a lot of German cooking. Because of the Depression, we'd pick fifty quarts of blueberries every year so have them canned for the rest of the year. We used to can tomatoes and beans and corn. Make sauerkraut.

They were just good, local, old-fashioned parents. They used to play Pinochle every Saturday night with my uncle Ed and my aunt Frida. And my father was always fighting with my aunt Frida because she used to cheat playing Pinochle. They'd play, oh, three or four hours every Saturday night.

My mom never talked much about her heritage. She came from a large family. I had an uncle Peter and an uncle John and an aunt Frida and an aunt Isobel. All German names and all just good people.

15

McDonald's Bar, 1910. Mac's dad second from left in white cap. Skidoo Macdonnell, black moustache. He returned to Ireland and died in 1946.

We didn't have indoor plumbing in our house until I got out of the army in '44 when I was 22 years old. We used to take our baths in a washtub in the kitchen. But when we got to be around eleven years old, we used to go down to the shifting shanty where the coal miners used to change their clothes before they'd come home from work. The man in charge used to let the kids go in as long as we behaved. We'd line up with the coal miners, taking our Saturday showers and then running home like hell.

We didn't have any supermarkets. We used to go to Camillo DeAngeli's, the store where you're on the book.

Everybody had a book. Whatever groceries you bought were marked down in the book. Then when the release check, or the welfare check, or paycheck, or whatever check would come in, you'd go up to Camillo's and pay the bill. And if you couldn't pay it all, that was all right. Because in those days, in Archbald, everybody was poor except two or three families that were so-called the "elite."

I enjoyed school.

My first grade class at St. Thomas Aquinas in Archbald was the first in the school's history, and I graduated from the eighth grade in June, 1935. I was a member of the 1939 graduating class of Archbald High School.

I was a fair student. I could have been better, but I was fair. (I still hold the school record for the number of 70s on my report card, thanks to teachers A. J. Burke, Peg Spillane, Mary O'Hara, Margaret Dougher, and Beatrice Cawley.) I became an Eagle Scout in 1939 as well. In a troop of 46, only Gerald Foote and I didn't have uniforms. Gerald was later killed in World War II.

In September 1939 I enrolled at St. Thomas Commercial School, which was located in the convent of the Immaculate Heart of Mary (IHM) order. The courses included typing, business, shorthand, accounting, and others, all for tuition of four dollars a month! Sister Jean was a teacher at the school. I recall the day I questioned her about an accounting problem, insisting that her solution was wrong. Her response was, "If you're wrong it will cost you!" She was correct, and my 100% grade fell to 50%.

My classmate Bessie Loftus was always late. My seat was in the last row near the door, and when Bessie would try to slip in quietly, I'd move my arm so she would bump it with the door!

During this term at the school I earned $16 a month working for Archbald Borough on a New Deal program sponsored by the National Recovery Administration (NRA) in response to the Great Depression. Pete Cawley was the foreman/truck driver. My assignment was Borough Road, we picked up garbage, cleaned the roads and basins and everything else. We got twenty-four dollars a month and four dollars of that went to my tuition.

The WPA guy used to give us a ride to basketball games in the open trucks. Then he started charging us a quarter. Once I went home for the money and it was the only time in my life that I saw my mother cry. She didn't have a quarter. Sister Jaque called my friend Johnny Murphy's father, and he came in with the quarter. We went up to the Maryknoll School for future priests in Clarks Summit and we knocked the hell out of them.

1938, Archbald High School junior. Third string guard. Only photo with hair!

- A Mac Story -

I returned from World War II for Christmas. After the usual family excitement On Christmas afternoon I called an old girlfriend who had written to me weekly during my tour with the Army. She was very pleasant and suggested that I come to Carbondale the next afternoon.

She told me then that she had met someone from the Upper Valley. He was the same size and had the same personality as me. She was going to marry him.

No Dear John letter—just a pleasant "I'm sorry." I wished her luck. Thank God, because otherwise I wouldn't have had Isobel.

First Jobs

THERE was no work available in the area after graduation. At Christmas time my Granduncle Bill, assistant postmaster in Scranton, found part-time jobs on the midnight shift for me, Jim Nolan, and Pinky Sullivan. We sorted mail by hand. If we came across a Christmas card addressed to a friend or anyone we knew, we'd put it in the California or Texas mailbag for a joke. Sometimes the card would arrive three weeks later!

I got another job as well. My uncle Ed Cawley was a supervisor for the A & P grocery stores in the Archbald area and Carbondale, and he was able to get me part-time work. The store managers were Gerry Gilroy, Tom Williamson and Hank Williamson. On my first day in Carbondale I was assigned to the cellar to bag fifteen-pound pecks of potatoes. The potatoes would pour down a chute from a tractor trailer. After a couple of hours, it became obvious that not every customer would be getting a fifteen-pound bag—some would get eleven pound bags, some twelve. The lucky ones would get seventeen pounds of potatoes. We'd just quit weighing them—it was much easier that way. I also worked part-time at the Globe Department Store in Scranton, unloading bed mattresses from a train onto a truck for delivery to the Globe warehouse.

After a while, in the fall of 1940, Jim Nolan, Pinky Sullivan and I decided to join the Army. Neither my mom or my dad would sign the papers, so Jim and Pinky went alone. It isn't like now, and I don't begrudge those guys who go over to Iraq and get to come home for two weeks after six months or a year. Jim and Pinky were over there for 47 consecutive months.

They spent 47 consecutive months overseas during World War II, most of the time in Greenland, before going to France and Germany. After their return to Archbald, it was common for them to say, "I was born in Archbald, but raised overseas."

Later, Jimmy Newcomb and I went to the Picatinny Arsenal in New Jersey, and we were hired after standing in line for hours. I was assigned as a messenger and given a two-wheel bike—I had to learn how to ride it because I'd never had one. We lived in the Wharton Hotel with fifteen other Picatinny workers from Archbald, including Junior Scanlon, Shake Keough, Peg Spillane and Anna Pete Burke. Peg and Anna took a leave of absence from high school teaching to help the war effort.

When we were able to come home on a weekend, Junior Scanlon charged $5 for the return trip in his car. We used to come home on Thursday nights once in a while as well, to go to the Dime Dance put on by the Knights of Columbus.

After the messenger job I was recruited by Ireland native Jim Convery to work in the experimental high explosives section. This brought more money and overtime. It was a great experience, but some weekends I'd come home a different color—yellow, red, pure white.

We worked on the second floor of the building. On our first day, they showed us how to use the emergency chutes which extended from the fire exits to the ground. We only had to use them once during the short time I worked in the department.

I learned afterward that my brother Tom was in the army and that my brother Mark would be going soon. I reported to George Wetherby at the draft board to join the service.

In the field in France

WAR

O<small>N</small> June third, 1943, I boarded a train for processing in Indiantown Gap along with "Feets" Barrett and thirty other friends from Archbald. I was assigned to an ammunition company in Texas. I was delighted to be sent to Texas, but when I arrived I realized that it wasn't a manufacturing plant like Picatinny, but rather a company of soldiers delivering ammunition to the battlefield. While I was waiting for basic training to start, I was called into the First Sergeant's office, scared that I had done something wrong. It was a very short interview.

The Sergeant growled, "Your records indicate you can type, right?"

"Yes, SIR!"

"Pack your baggage. You are going to Savannah, Illinois, for ten weeks of training as a detachment clerk." [like the character Radar O'Reilly in MASH] The good part was ten weekends in nearby Chicago where everything was *free.*

I went to see Captain Mullen, MD and Captain Korner for approval. After a two-minute interval I was back in the barracks packing my bags. I was off to Savannah. After a series of bus and train rides I was ready to learn Army clerical work.

I was assigned to a medical detachment as a clerk because I was the only one in the group that had any academic training or office training. And because it was composed of four officers, four doctors, seven enlisted men and we stayed together. We shipped out of New York on December 26th of 1944. They wouldn't even let us get outside on the ship to see the Statue of Liberty.

But we shipped out and we went to England where we trained. And then I guess the next point in my career was D-Day + six. I went into Normandy, as a combat medic. It was quite a scene, quite an effort. And as the troops moved ahead further, we kept moving along with them. Finally we were stationed in a town called Soissons which had a huge railroad rail yard where all the ammunition trains used to come in. It was during the Battle of the Bulge. One German plane bombed our rail head and it was probably the biggest 4th of July display you'll ever see in your life. It was at the point that I was awarded a Bronze Star for my help evacuating, taking care of civilians, soldiers.

During that period of time we used to ride shotgun with the Red Truck Express. It was hauling explosives up into the Battle of the Bulge. I prayed more there than I ever did before or since in my life.

The war changed me. For one thing, I lost my hair. I had a greater sense of responsibility. It wasn't war-related, but I delivered three babies by myself, because the doctors were busy doing other things and these French women just came in and ...that was an experience. It was scary. Scary, even though we knew the doctors were nearby.

Seeing people and realizing how lucky we were gave me a great desire to help people. I think that's probably where I found my desire for public service.

Would I have done it over again, enlisted? At a drop of a hat.

The Scranton Times

BY JOSH MCAULIFFE (STAFF WRITER)
Published: November 14, 2010

Francis X. "Mac" McDonnell never fired a gun in his life. But you don't need to pack heat to be a war hero.

On the day after Christmas, 1944, Mr. McDonnell, a combat medic for the 1st Army's 166th Battalion, helped save the lives of a number of soldiers and civilians injured during a German bombing raid over a railroad ammunition depot in Soissons, France. His heroics earned him a Bronze Star.

"Biggest fireworks you ever saw in your life," said Mr. McDonnell, 88, of Jessup, a private first class at the time of the bombing who was later promoted to staff sergeant.

That's but one of many instances in which the Archbald native lent a helping hand to his fellow GIs.

Prewar choices
Looking back on Mr. McDonnell's life, it's interesting to see how fortuitous his prewar experiences proved to be.

After graduating from the old Archbald High School, Mr. McDonnell took courses in bookkeeping, accounting and shorthand at the former St. Thomas Commercial School. Then, in 1940, he went to work at the Picatinny Arsenal in Dover, N.J. A laborer in the plant's High Explosives (HE) department, one of the first things he learned to do was operate the chute system that got employees out of the building in the event of an explosion.

"You'd come some weekends and be yellow. The next weekend, green. The next weekend, blue," Mr. McDonnell said, only half-jokingly.

He came home one weekend in early 1943 to find that his brothers Tom and Mark had both been drafted. "So I went down to the draft board and said, 'Hey, I want in,'" he said.

Mr. McDonnell's first stop was Texas, where he joined the 166th Battalion. Shortly after arriving, he was called into the first sergeant's office. First thing the sergeant asked him was, "Can you type?"

When he said yes, he was promptly given a transfer to Savanna, Ill., to take Army business courses. Among the highlights of his stint there were the weekend trips to Chicago, where servicemen didn't have to pay for a thing.

By the time he got back to Texas, the 166th had already moved on. A few days later, he caught up with the unit in Louisiana, and was made company clerk of the battalion's medical detachment.

"So while everyone else was out on maneuvers, I was in the dispensary tent counting aspirins," he said with a laugh.

From there, it was on to Europe. Mr. McDonnell was based in the forests of Marlborough, England, for a few months before heading to France in the weeks following the Normandy invasion on D-Day. His medical unit was attached to a battalion that supplied ammunition to the artillery and infantry. Mr. McDonnell was in charge of maintaining the unit's records, including the daily sick call.

Given that he was far from the front lines, Mr. McDonnell didn't witness any truly ghastly combat injuries in the course of his deployment. Mostly, his unit dealt with minor, treatable maladies. For instance, there was the time he had to check an entire company of soldiers, most of whom were ex-convicts, for venereal disease by using a technique called "short-arming."

Another day, Allied Commander Gen. Dwight D. Eisenhower visited the camp, and Mr. McDonnell was charged with fetching aspirin for the general's chauffeur, Kay Summersby.

"In Korea, I would have been Radar O'Reilly," Mr. McDonnell said, referencing the popular character on the long-running television series, "M*A*S*H," which was set in an Army medical unit during the Korean War.

"I never had it bad," he said. "When I say I was lucky, I mean it."

In times of peril, though, he ably proved his bravery.

This was especially true on the night of Dec. 26, 1944, when a German pilot began raining bombs on top of Soissons. One of his targets was a rail yard where the Americans were storing a significant amount of bombs and other heavy ammunition. It was one of the biggest operations of its kind on the continent, Mr. McDonnell said.

One of the train cars exploded, and within minutes the fire had spread to the other cars, as well as the nearby homes.

"It was just like if you bombed Wyoming and Lackawanna avenues," Mr. McDonnell said.

Quickly, Mr. McDonnell and other members of his unit mobilized, running into the flaming rail yard, shrapnel flying all around them, with stretchers and First Aid kits. They did it over and over again throughout the night and into the next day.

A lot of people, military personnel and civilians alike, were injured. However, the deaths were minimal.

Was he scared?

"Yeah, you're always scared," Mr. McDonnell said.

Mr. McDonnell's good deeds didn't go unrecognized. In addition to the Bronze Star, which he earned for what his commanding officer called an "utter disregard for his own safety," he received a commendation from the people of Soissons.

A year later, on Christmas Eve, 1945, Mr. McDonnell returned to Archbald. That night, he went out and tipped back a few with two of his best friends, who also had just returned from long tours of duty.

The next morning, he came home to find the bottle of champagne he had brought back from France half empty. His father, Patrick, had sampled some.

"He said, 'That's the worst damn thing I ever had in my life. It tasted like vinegar,'" Mr. McDonnell said.

Unlike his father, Mr. McDonnell was able to avoid a life in the mines when his uncle helped get him a job with the state Bureau of Employment and Security. He eventually rose to become its regional director, retiring in 1998 at age 76. To this day, he still fields calls from people looking for advice on how to get a job.

"I loved going to work every day of my life," he said.

Often, his job included helping fellow veterans find work. In the late 1950s, he created the American Legion's

Employment Program, which was implemented on a national level.

Mr. McDonnell's other veterans affairs activities include membership in the Kentucky Colonels, Chapel of the Four Chaplains, Jessup Veterans of Foreign Wars and the Ambrose Revels American Legion Post 328, Archbald.

Meanwhile, he was a close friend of the late Gino Merli, the World War II veteran and Medal of Honor recipient from Peckville. Mr. Merli visited Mr. McDonnell in the hospital just days before he passed away in 2002.

Today, Mr. Merli's Medal of Honor sits in the Gino Merli Room at Valley Community Library in Peckville, which Mr. McDonnell helped establish and continues to maintain.

His has been a life of service, and a good one at that.

"I've had a great run," he said.

ARCHBALD SOLDIER AWARDED BRONZE STAR FOR HEROISM

With the Oise Supply Section in France (By Mail).— For disregarding his own safety and evacuating casualties from a fireswept ammunition depot railyard, Pvt. Francis X. McDonnell, of 313 South Main Street, Archbald, Pa., was decorated with the Bronze Star.

Private McDonnell was one of fifteen officers and enlisted men who received the award from Brig. Gen. C. O. Thrasher, commanding general of Oise Supply Section.

The citation accompanying the award reads in part: "Private McDonnell, without regard for personal safety, remained at his post as first aid man and litter bearer, and evacuated casualties at the railyard which was bombed and strafed by an enemy plane. The heroic efforts and exceptional devotion to duty displayed by Private McDonnell reflect the highest credit on him and the armed forces of the United States."

VILLE DE SOISSONS
OFFICE OF THE MAYOR

The people of the City Soissons are very gratified of your good conduct at the time of the explosions of the ammunition wagons at the station by an enemy aircraft the 26th of December, 1944.

Thanks to your courage and disregard for danger some irreplaceable losses have been averted.

I am very happy in the name of the City Soissons to offer you this medal and souvenir of our great appreciation.

Mayor of Soissons

Dear Francis X:

I couldn't buy a Sunday paper last Sunday....When I did, I understood why. I knew that you were a decorated Veteran, who graduated form Archbald High School. What I didn't know was that you are a decorated Medic.

Congratulations on a great article....We are all very proud of you.

Judge Robert A. Mazzoni

*Sleigh riding in Soisson on a homemade sled with
the kids in the area, 1944*

Family cruise after my retirement

Isobel and the Children

Jim Nolan, Pinky Sullivan and I were sitting in the American Legion on a Saturday night. We decided to go down the road to Munley's Bar. Isobel and Mary Donnelly were drinking Cokes in the back room. I had gone to school with Mary, so I joined them. Mary introduced me to Isobel and the rest, as they say, is history.

A couple nights later, I called her and asked her if she'd like to go out and she wasn't too happy about that. She asked me who I thought I was, calling her on a Saturday night. As though she wouldn't have a date already! So I apologized and said I'd talk to her again and she said "Well, I'm not doing anything Monday or Tuesday night." She had a steady boyfriend at that time. And that was it.

She was attractive, nice, very personable, good conversationalist. I think I grew on her like a wart. After she met me, her mother asked, "Where did you find that buck?" But after a time Isobel's mother said to her, "Mac would dig ditches to put pork chops on your table." We had fifty-nine wonderful years of life together (and I didn't have to dig any ditches.)

- A Mac Story -

When Isobel was co-owner of the Colonial Flower Shop in Olyphant, we used to use peonies in our Easter baskets. They weren't in bloom yet—we had to put them in water and wait for them to bloom. We took the buckets of peonies and put them in Polly Ward's apartment over the flower shop.

A woman came pick out peonies. When we went upstairs, we saw that Polly had opened her oven so the warmth would bring the flowers into beautiful bloom.

We lost our first our first son. He was stillborn.

That had a drastic effect on both Isobel and myself. We then had a daughter Ellen, and that was a shock. A good shock, of course. We lost another son at eight months. Then we had Erin. We lost another boy, at six months. And then we had Marty, and life had never been the same. And then we had Elizabeth and it's been a great joy.

Ellen graduated from Penn State and then earned a Master's degree. She works for National Public Radio. Erin finished at East Stroudsburg and has been employed at Keystone Resources. Currently, she's a manager at a group home. Marty attended Vo-Tech and Johnson College and is employed by the Pennsylvania Department of Transportation.

Elizabeth graduated from Lackawanna College

and is currently employed by the state workman's compensation. I have the four best kids in the world. Going up to Moosic Lake with our kids, taking them down to park, just watching them grow up. Their successes, whatever failures they had, I was always there for them.

I try to be a good father, I think I have been. On a scale of one to ten, I probably would get up to an eight or nine, maybe. My dream for my children is that they be happy in what they do. If it makes them happy, that's good enough for me.

- A Mac Story -

Ellen got her driver's license, and we used to let her take the car to high school in Dunmore. One night we had a snowstorm and she walked in. I asked her, "How was the driving?"

And she said, "Oh, it was tough, Dad. The car's down on Moosic Street in the snow bank." She just ran into the snow bank, left the car, and walked home.

WBRE
ALL NEWS RADIO

July 15, 1977

To Ellen McDonnel with all the union copies.

Dear Ellen:

We regret to inform you that we shall not require your services beyond the probationary period which ends on July 18.

This is in no way a reflection upon your attitude or your desire to do a good job in your assigned ppsition. The difficult combination of technical and vocal skills necessary for successfully meeting the needs of our station have not been met by you during this time. As we have counseled with you during this period, it was our hope that there would be sufficient improvement in your performance to warrant continuance as a permanent staff member, but there has been no consistent quality of performance.

We shall be happy to recommend you for your cooperative nature, diligence in pursuing assigned tasks, your writing ability, and attendence.

Sincerely,

Joseph B. Gries
Station/Sales Manager

JBG/ab

cc: Hayes
    Koff
    B. Oliver
    Gries

Dad, save this. Some day when I'm network, I'll send it to Joseph B. Gries.

I found this letter in the attic. Many years later, when Ellen became a producer at NPR, it was used to inspire young job applicants.

From the Website of National Public Radio: *Ellen McDonnell is NPR's Executive Editor of News Programming, responsible for overseeing all of NPR's news programs: Morning Edition, All Things Considered, Talk of the Nation, Tell Me More and Weekend Edition.*

- A Mac Story -

In those days it was common to use laurel as a filler in flower arrangements. Sometimes, the farmer wouldn't come around with any so I had to go up on the mountain and get some myself. This time I sent my son Marty up, and it had snowed.Now it's illegal to pick laurel, so I told Marty to stay off the main road. Anyway, he pulled off Route 247, and a state trooper saw him. "What are you doing in there, son?" "I'm looking for my class ring!" The trooper said, "Good luck!" and just drove away.

Isobel's brother John invited
us to a Halloween party at
the Elkview Country Club.
Alice Reap volunteered to
make me a costume. I said,
"You make it and I'll wear
it." I wore it to the party with
pink shoes and won first
prize. Some of my friends
have since borrowed it.

Rockingham Park, 1962. Isobel bet on "Finegan's Wake," but he dropped dead, in first place, in the stretch!

Isobel and PA Secretary of Labor Tom Foley. She's not slapping him--it's just a pat as she's telling a story!

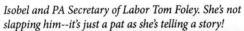

For My Wife
ON VALENTINE'S DAY

Valentine Isobel kept
until her death

*F*or years, you've been
the last person I see each night
before I go to sleep
and the first person I see
each day when I wake up...
Even after all this time,
I still think that's the nicest way
to begin and end my day.

Happy Valentine's Day

Love
Jak

Dear Mac —

Mostly of all I'd like to say "thank you" for all the times I've failed to say "thank you."

Thank you for the fresh raspberries in the morning and the delicious orange marmalade!

Thank you for never forgetting our special dates and events.

Thank you for your cheerful attitude and for never being angry with me (even when I deserved it) or saying an unkind word about anyone.

Thank you for always being there — in good times — in trying times —and most of all during the diffucult times we have experienced.

Thank you for the wonderful loving care you take of our family— Ellen, Erin, Marty, Elizabeth, and all our dear grandchildren.

Thank you for your devotion to our Veterans — the unemployed and the disadvantaged — and for your special slogan that "Every Day is Veteran's Day" at your offices.

Thank you for your spirit of generosity!

May God bless your retirement and grant you a long and healthy and happy life.

May God keep you from all physical and moral harm, for we love you dearly.

Isobel and the kids

Our 35th Anniversary
We would like to share
With family and friends
We hope you will be there.

We had a good life
And would like to celebrate
Sunday, July 26
Is the date.

You might have had
Tennis or a golf match planned.
Or maybe a swim and picnic
We understand.

But for this special event
A party is our plan.
You are a special friend
We hope you can be on hand.

St. James Church, Jessup PA
Is the place to be
Mass will be celebrated at 3:30 p.m.
By Father Mark Connolly, C.P.

Then to Montdale
For cocktails at five
Much of this celebration
To Isobel is a surprise!

Your invitation comes in rhyme
Our answer does the same
The Pennsylvania hills we'll climb
For Jessup we'll take aim

We'll put aside our fun and games
Forget the park and beach
And point the car toward Old St. James
In time, the Mass to reach

The Pennsylvania Pike we'll take
To our Jessup destination
And leaving beautiful Spring Lake
We'll join the celebration

We're pleased to be invited
We'll make the trip and back
Who wouldn't be delighted
To honor Is and Mac?

Respecting your desires
To keep it a surprise
We aren't good as liars
But no one we'll put wise

And now the time has come to say
How glad we'll be to share
Your Thirty-Fifth—a special day
God willing, we'll be there!

—John Bergin, Saint Peter's College

49 *John recently came into our lives. His*
mother was my dad's first cousin.

From a homily delivered at 35th Anniversary Mass by Erin McDonnell:

Of the three cardinal virtues, Faith is the first. My parents at their wedding could not bear to stand before God and recite their wedding vows, if they did not feel such devout faith and did not have such a firm hope that their love was strong enough to keep them. And going through life's journey, they could never keep going if they did not believe that God is with them all the way.

I know my parents have a strong love for each other that was experienced by myself and my brother and sisters. We all experienced a love that is gentle and firm. All of us had love poured into us. It's constant, kind, and firm.

We knew from when we got up in the morning that our parents wanted the best for us, and did their best to make sure we had everything.

Because I came later in the marriage, I found I got away with a lot of things the others never did. I'm lucky not only for having two parents who give without counting the cost. I hope we have them for the next 35 years, and if we do, I'll be just as grateful to them as I am now.

- A Mac Story -

I always put my Thanksgiving turkey in an oiled brown paper bag to cook, just the way my mother used to. Nice and moist. One year, I wasn't ready to cook the turkey, but it was cold outside. We had a swing out on the back porch, so I went out and set the turkey on the swing. One of Erin's college classmates came to visit, and she asked, "Mr. McDonnell, how come your turkey is on the back porch?" I answered, "It relaxes the turkey before we put it in the oven!" What makes the story funnier is that she told her mother, and her mother called Isobel and asked her, "How long does Mac leave the turkey out on the swing?" Isobel just said, "I don't know, I really don't know."

- A Mac Story -

Last summer I was making breakfast for Isobel. I set out our morning vitamins. After a few minutes, Isobel said, "Mac, you forgot one of your pills." I reached over and popped it in my mouth. Isobel suddenly gasped, "You swallowed my hearing aid!" Well, it was tiny and looked just like a vitamin pill.

I quickly called Dr. Majernick and went to Mid-Valley Hospital for an X-ray. The hearing aid was there in my throat on its way to my stomach. X-rays for the next seven days before it...surfaced. I wanted to clean it up and have it repaired, but Isobel said, "Not in my ear!" So $300 later she got her new hearing aid.

Father Mark with Ellen

With Cardinal Cooke

Father Mark

FAITH

I met Father Mark Connolly around June 15 in 1957. He was coming down the hall in Mercy Hospital in Scranton. I stopped Father Mark and asked him to come in and bless Isobel, who was a patient at the time. After a short visit he told us that he was due back at the monastery by 6 p.m. I then asked him to come to Jessup for dinner at our house. He stated that he needed permission from the Provincial, because he couldn't fraternize with parishioners. I answered that I belonged to Saint James in Jessup. He asked me to call in a few days.

I called and he agreed to come at noon on a Thursday—he'd take a bus. I told him I'd pick him up.

This was the start of a friendship that has lasted to this day and will go on FOREVER.

Every Thursday I'd pick up Father Mark for dinner, usually at my home or a local restaurant. Afterwards we'd watch The Untouchables from 9 to 10 p.m., then, back to the monastery. This continued until Father was transferred to Riverdale, New York with Saint Michael's parish in Greenwich. In 1986 he had a series of meetings with New York's Cardinal Cooke, resulting in a televised Mass on Channel 9. We were guests of Father Mark and Father Leo when they celebrated Christmas and Easter Mass. We were always guests of the Cardinal at Christmas and Easter Mass until his death; then, Cardinal O'Connor followed the tradition. On one occasion Father Mark asked me to bring an Easter basket for Cardinal O'Connor.

The second Easter I had some friends in the Carbondale office bring in some colored eggs, most of which had come from Russia and other Eastern European countries, to present to the Cardinal. I joked to him, "Don't throw away the shells!" He recognized the craftsmanship involved and how valuable the eggs were.

- A Mac Story -

Father Conniff became the pastor of our church here at Saint James about 30 years ago. He came to see me about getting some poinsettias for the church, but he wanted to go to the greenhouse in Pittston and pick out his own. The greenhouse had about 6000, but Father Conniff only wanted 50. The owner was a big, tall lanky guy--I just shrugged, and he took us through the whole greenhouse. Father would just point and say, "I'll take that one, and that one, and that one..." Now, they're all the same, but he picked out 50 one at a time, and come Christmas we delivered them. Father Conniff said, "Now, don't they look nice? Isn't it great that you can pick out your own?"

April 13, 1988

Dear Mac and Isobel,

I understand that you were responsible for the lovely Easter basket that was presented to me at the taping of the Easter Mass....It's nice to know my friends in Scranton have not forgotten me—I certainly will always remember them.

With gratitude for your thoughtfulness and assuring you of a remembrance in my prayers, I am

Faithfully in Christ,

John Cardinal O'Connor
Archbishop of New York

March 3, 1981

Sincere thanks for your thoughtful greeting and very generous gift on the fiftieth anniversary of my priesthood, You're much too kind and generous with me....I must say, "Thank you, God, for length of years, a healthy life, an extended preaching apostolate and above all else, a host of dear friends. This makes me just about the richest and luckiest man in North America. And now, the new John Paul may smile more, but he can't be happier or more contented than Clem.

Again, sincere thanks, and hurry back to visit us. May God always bless you.

Devotedly,

Father Clement Buckley, C. P

(Father Mark's friend)

July 19, 2006

Thank you for your generosity for my farewell from the Vicar ministry. Be well, and know that the jelly jars are already in circulation in Monroe County.

Peace in Christ,

Father Joe Kopacz

(Former Pastor at St. James and still our long-time friend. He attends Ellen's Christmas party at home every year.)

"EVERY DAY WAS VETERANS DAY" – John Gilhool, Jim Nolan,
Carbondale LO-Church Street   Frank McDonnell, Tom Toolan
and Ed Stratford

Launch of the Veteran's Day program at the Carbondale Job Center

Job Center

THE war was over. After several weeks at home, signing for the fifty-two twenty club at the unemployment office in Archbald, I wanted a job. I talked to my dad about a job at the Eddy Creek mine in Olyphant. His reply? "NOT in the mines! End of conversation."

After daily coaxing he agreed to find me something safe. Several weeks later I was told that I'd soon be starting as a company laborer with Johnny Gaughan, whom my dad deemed "a highly safe miner." You got to realize that my father was picking slate at the age of seven. He lost his mother and father in the same month when he was eleven and he was his only support for his brothers and sisters.

I was thrilled, and I walked up to Aunt Rose's house to tell her the good news. Her reply was simple: "No nephew of mine is going to work in the mines!" So, she woke up her husband, who worked in the Carbondale employment office, and asked him if there were any jobs available other than in the mines. His reply was that the state was going to open a new employment office in Olyphant. With my experience as a Medical Detachment clerk and commercial school graduate, I might qualify.

Early the next morning I rode the bus ride to Olyphant, complete with an Honorable Discharge. I stood in line with hundreds of GIs until I got inside and told the Personnel receptionist that I desired to work in the new office. He took me in to see Gerald Lynett, who advised me to contact Army Personnel at Picatinny arsenal in Dover, New Jersey and get a release. The next day I took the Greyhound to Dover and had an interview with a Mrs. Burns, who drew up the necessary paperwork. Next day, back to Olyphant and the long line to see Mr. Lynett.

My running around paid off. I started work on March 5, 1946 at $1238 per year, giving up my 52/20 $20 weekly ($1040 a year).

It was the greatest break of my life. I wound up fifty-six years with the state agency, including serving as regional director for the last ten years of my career.

The saga continues....The bus left Archbald at 8:10, arriving at Blakely Corners at 8:30. I had to walk three-quarters of a mile to the office. There was a bus home leaving Blakely Corners at 5:00 p.m., but the walk back required me to wait for the next bus at 5:30.

I was promoted to Senior Clerk on April 4, 1946 at $1738 per year. More promotions on October 31 raised me to $2268 per year and to $2820 on September 16, 1949. By July 16, 1952, I was earning $3420 a year.

A letter on September 1, 1964 notified me to report to the Carbondale Office in two days. This was part of a management switch—McCarty to Olyphant, me to Carbondale, Kornish to Pittston, Peter to Scranton. What a surprise! There had been no warning. I reported to supervisors Lucille Coyle and Charles Biglin, both of them long, longtime employees. I was responsible for offices in Forest City, Susquehanna, New Milford and Montrose. I traveled to various school districts to schedule GATB aptitude tests.

The staff was glad to see me, but not the two supervisors.

I was then the youngest manager in the state in the Department of Labor. And I enjoyed it; I had many, many happy days. I was able to help literally thousands of people.

I had lived through the sewing industry, the shoe industry, the mining industry, and there wasn't much work to be had. You'd have to talk to people, and try to help them best you can. Do whatever you could to help them. I've devoted my life, I guess, to community service, maybe at some times neglecting my family, I don't know.

I always told everybody who wanted to look for a job not to depend on Career Link. Use everybody you have-- your friends, your relatives, your church, politicians. Anyone who will help you get a job. In my own experience, if I didn't go to see my Aunt Rose that night to tell her I was going to work in the mines, I wouldn't be writing this story. I'd be a retired coal miner, or probably dead twenty-five years ago. I had a lot of jobs. I was hired as a bike messenger in New Jersey, and I didn't even know how to ride a bike! As a kid, I didn't even have a two-wheeled bike, so I had to learn to ride one.

Lives Touched by Mac

Gerry Roback's husband died of a heart attack at the age of 48 and left two small children. Gerry was an excellent employee at the Carbondale Job Center, but she was considering leaving her job so that she could get her kids on the school bus every morning. I suggested changing her 8: 30 to 5:00 work schedule. She could start at 9:15 if she skipped her lunch hour and breaks. I didn't notify the regional or state office. All of Gerry's coworkers agreed to the change. Gerry eventually returned to her original schedule.

This policy of mine is now known everywhere as flextime. (Gerry's son Joe is now Assistant Vice-President in charge of Admissions at the University of Scranton; her daughter Cheryl is a teacher in the Lake Wallenpaupack School District.)

FRANCIS X. McDONNELL

SUMMARY OF QUALIFICATIONS

Distinguished career in public service with the PA Department of Labor and Industry, culminating with appointment in 1991 to position as Regional Director–Job Center Field Operations. Extensive experience in planning, directing, organizing and supervising a full range of employment training, unemployment compensation and supportive services in ten offices throughout an eight-county, 8,000-square-mile area in Northeastern PA.

SELECTED CAREER ACCOMPLISHMENTS

Implemented and directed the Commonwealth policies concerning the administration of the Job Service and Unemployment Compensation Programs. Working with Regional Staff, provided guidance and direction to local Job Centers in the Region.

Organized, coordinated and directed Regional Staff Technicians in assisting local Job Center Managers in establishing priorities, planning workload goals and measuring performance within the staff in establishing periodic reviews with each Job Center Manager to track progress and recommend corrective actions.

Inaugurated a Job Placement Program in Lackawanna County for individuals recovering from drug and alcohol addictions.

Developed and directed a plan for active participation with employers through Employer Advisory Councils (EACs). Established and maintained effective working relationships with other governmental agencies, and cooperative efforts of these agencies in developing the expansion of job opportunities and information on eligibility for AWAKE programs.

Developed a plan of service utilizing staff conferences, current performance evaluations, economic forecasts, and state office program. Established local office overall objectives fully utilizing staff resources to provide the maximum employment service, unemployment compensation and related activities to the individuals and employers in the communities served.

AREAS OF EXPERIENCE/KNOWLEDGE

Employment and Training • Unemployment Compensation • Employee Relations • Staff Development • Compliance with Federal and State Policies and Procedures • Community Relations and Resources • Labor-Management Relations

EMPLOYMENT HISTORY

12/98 to Present
- Consultant—Veterans, Drug/Alcohol
- Active Member, Scranton Lackawanna Human Development Agency
- Mid Valley Representative, Head Start Program

12/91 to 12/98
- Regional Director—Job Center Field Operations, PA Department of Labor and Industry, Region #8, Scranton

1/45 to 12/91
- Manager—Olyphant and Carbondale Job Centers, PA Department of Labor and Industry

MILITARY

- World War II Combat Medic, U.S. Army; Honorable Discharge, Bronze Star
- 166 Medical Detachment—Clerk (Radar)

EDUCATION

Professional development and continuing education at Michigan State University, Wharton School of Finance, Syracuse University, Pennsylvania State University, University of Scranton

COMMUNITY SERVICE AND AFFILIATIONS

Active in the following Community Service and Veterans Organizations:

- Past Commander—Ambrose Revels Post 328 American Legion
- Past Department of Pennsylvania Employment Chairman—American Legion
- Past Chairman—Upper NE Pennsylvania Governor's Committee for Employment of the Handicapped, 35 years
- Past Member—Valley View School District Advisory Committee
- Past Member–Chambers of Commerce, Carbondale, Scranton and Archbald
- International Association of Personnel in Employment Security (IAPES)
- Member and Past President—St. James of Jessup Combined Societies
- Past President—St. Joseph's Hospital Foundation Board

- Knights of Columbus–3rd and 4th degree
- Life Member Veterans of Foreign Wars/American Legion
- Member—Lackawanna County Vo-Tech Advisory Committee
- Member—Workforce Advisory Board
- Past Board Member and Secretary—Valley Community Library
- Co-Chairman—Gino Merli Medal of Honor Room
- Trustee—The Chapel of the Four Chaplains
- Member—Jessup Crime Watch Committee

AWARDS

- State VFW Award, 1971, 1972, 1977, 1978, 1979, 1980, 1981, 1983
- IAPES—Local Office—Veterans Placements, 1974, 1975
- State American Legion—Citation Award, 1976
- State DAV—Local Office Award, 1980
- State AMVETS, 1981
- Post 328 American Legion Life Member (Only one in history of Post), 1987
- IAPES—Employee Performance Award, 1988
- Arkansas Traveler, 1990
- VFW—Award Life Membership, 1991
- Kentucky Colonel, 1995
- Trustee, Chapel of the Four Chaplains
- Member, National WWII Museum, New Orleans
- Paralyzed Veterans of America, Certificate

June 12, 1987

Dear Frank:

Yesterday in the Sunday Times I read the article about the BES office in Carbondale and about you. This gives me an opportunity to say in no uncertain terms that there are many of us in the area who are eternally grateful to you for all the fine work you have done over so many years.

Our unemployment rate is way down and people can find work. So we are making progress.

Thanks again and again and again.

William W. Scranton

August 27, 2011

On retiring recently, I've had time to look back on my career, trying to sort out what it all meant, including those who have influenced my working life for the better, You naturally came to mind. I have never forgotten that my having the chance to prove myself as a workforce program professional and advance over the years owed much to your hiring me in the first place.

Awareness of my own job security always prompted me to do my best for the people we serve, following the good examples of public service and dedication to duty which you set for those working under you.

Tony Betti

A Life Touched by Mac

The Sunday Times

October 23, 1988

"Gary Clister is one of the success stories of the Trade Adjustment Assistance Program," explained Francis X. McDonnell, manager of the Carbondale Job Service Office.

"Here's a young man who worked in the coal mines. Four years later he has a good job as a field service engineer. Gary was able to receive extended unemployment benefits, training, and even relocation benefits," explained McDonnell. "This is one of the better programs that we offer. It gives workers the opportunity to learn new skills and to get back into the labor market."

A Life Touched by Mac

The Sunday Times

November 4, 1979

Francis X. McDonnell, when speaking of his old friend Jane Martens Carter, says she is "a great gal, lots of fun, a good person." But when McDonnell helped Joseph Quinn write a letter of recommendation for Mrs. Carter, who works from a wheelchair, to the President's Committee on Employment of the Handicapped, it came out this way:

"Jane Carter is a person who under the most adverse conditions has overcome a handicap to become a useful citizen and her own person. She is an inspiration to all who meet her. Through her employment at Allied Service, she is able to transmit silently her own philosophy of living to patients and coworkers."

As a result of the recommendation, Mrs. Carter was awarded a presidential citation for meritorious service.

Sept. 22, 1972

It is never too late to thank those who have contributed so much to help us overcome the ravages caused by Hurricane Agnes in Northeastern Pennsylvania. Without the help of you and your devoted staff it would have been impossible for our Luzerne Bureau of Employment Security offices to overcome the overwhelming odds that confronted us.

Again, accept our sincerest gratitude for helping us serve the public during this emergency.

Guy Solfanelli, District Manager #3

My team and I worked from June 27 to Labor Day during the summer of Agnes. As a reward (instead of cash) we were given sixteen days of comp time in late November to be used by the end of the year.

I'd do it again—I volunteered during another hurricane years later, but I was told that I was too old!

I had the west side of the river. Billy "Kelly" Lalley had the east side of the river (a great guy and an excellent employee). Kelly later became a State Director (my boss at the time).

One day he called the Regional Office looking for me. Jane Carter said, "He's on the way to Montrose. I'll call Isobel."

Jane called him back. "I don't have his cell phone number."

Upon my arrival in Montrose I called Kell. My cell phone wasn't made to accept calls--just make outgoing cals. After a brief discussion Kelly told me he was going to get the same cell phone for himself! End of story.

𝔖crantonian
June, 1967

BES Hunting Jobless With Bus Equipment

The BES is now using a bus equipped with an office to ride out to meet and deal with the jobless. The new type of bus office has been operative at Hallstead, Forest City, Montrose, Susquehanna, and Newfoundland and is currently assigned to Frank McDonnell, manager of the Carbondale office.

This is how we spent the summer of '67—men only!

June 30, 1971

OUT OF THE CELLAR AND INTO THE LIGHT!

The Susquehanna Bureau of Employment Service has changed its location. As of today the new office is located in the renovated Charles Brown Hardware Store, East Main Street.

Mr. Frances X. McDonnell, Manager of the Carbondale and Susquehanna BES office said, "We are now in our new quarters with new facilities and added personnel which will greatly increase the office production."

The entire move was completed in twenty minutes with the help of employees from "Operation Mainstream."

The Sunday Times

Friday, May 4, 1974

How well the Carbondale Bureau of Employment Security office has tackled the problem of assisting veterans was recognized when, for an unprecedented second time in as many years it received the Veterans of Foreign Wars' Statewide Award for providing "outstanding service" to veterans. The award will be presented to Mr. Francis McDonnell and his staff at a dinner at Runco's Inn, Dunmore.

A U.S. veterans employment representative said, "This office is providing veterans with an outstanding program of services. There is no doubt that the program of services for veterans is the most important of all programs in the Carbondale Office.

It is most gratifying to note that an office of this size, located in one of the higher unemployment areas of the state, has established a highly effective program for the employment of veterans. This has not come about by chance. It has come through the diligent efforts of the manager, the veterans' employment representative, and the entire local staff. This performance demonstrates that regardless of local conditions, an outstanding program for veterans can be developed. In comparison, other local offices in more advantageous localities have not been able to show this kind of motivation."

April 29, 1992

Genetti's Manor, Dickson City

*Pennsylvania Region No. 8
Job Center
and
Scranton Lackawanna Human
Development Agency
Salute*

Francis X. McDonnell

Invocation and Benediction—Rev. Mark Connolly

**Pledge of Allegiance—Gino Merli,
Congressional Medal of Honor Recipient**

**Toastmaster—Austin Burke, President,
Greater Scranton Chamber of Commerce**

Remarks—Ellen McDonnell Stevens

A career employee of Labor and Industry since 1946, he has been the Manager of the Carbondale Job Center for 27 years.

Mac has been active in service to the communities of the upvalley and to the Veterans of Pennsylvania. Founder of the Veterans Award Dinner sponsored by the Carbondale Job Center, he has always promoted Veterans' programs and worked diligently for Veterans.

His untiring efforts to assist recovering alcoholics and drug addicts throughout the Carbondale Job Center have benefitted many in regaining and/or establishing productive and meaningful lives.

As Director of Region 8 Job Center Field Operations, Mac will direct nine full-service Job Centers and three unemployment compensation claims offices that serve more than 840,000 people and over 17,000 employers covering Lackawanna, Luzerne, Schuylkill, Bradford, Tioga, Wyoming, Sullivan, and Susquehanna Counties.

It is with much enthusiasm that Mac takes on this latest challenge of his career. His efforts in supporting the Veterans, the Handicapped, and the Unemployed will merely be extended to a larger area. All of Region 8 has gained a friend.

Dec. 5, 1993

Mac,

I want to thank you for your support and direction in getting approval for my participation in the ODAP training in Hershey.

Not only was I inspired and educated, but I feel my work and our program for recovering people was validated. Two other participants in the training were past clients from our fledgling days in Carbondale.

The whole session was enlightening and rewarding on many levels.

Thanks again,

Bob Davis

Oct. 19, 2006

Dear Mac,

Just in case I never told you, I appreciate all you have done for me since I started with the state. The "Old Soldier" has and always will be a cherished mentor and, above all, a friend. Semper Fidelis.

Mike McLane

Aug. 4, 1998

Mac,

I hope you're getting some relaxation and enjoyment since you've left the trenches. After all you have done for so many people, you certainly are entitled.

I can never express to you how grateful I am for the chances you have given me and the faith you had in me when I didn't.

I believe that we have really had an impact on the lives of many recovering people, and I am carrying on the program using much of inspiration you gave.

Thanks for teaching me about patience, faith, dedication and perseverence. Enjoy!

Bob D.

Dear Frank,

I have the job with Head Start. I would like to thank you because I know I would not have been so fortunate without your help.

Thank you again,

Judy Rogan

Aug. 20, 1993

Dear Mr. McDonnell:

I would like to take a moment to thank you for the excellent job I was able to acquire. I will commence training as a carpenter's apprentice on Aug. 23. Without efforts by so many people, my employment status was not very promising. I just wanted to extend my deepest thanks.

Denise McLaud

July 1, 1997

Colonel,

Thank you for your help and your kindness. I sincerely appreciate the opportunity to work, and to retrain myself in order to earn a living outside a kitchen.

Although my hearing loss is severe, at the Job Center I feel that the problem is understood and worked with rather than against. I know this is in large part due to your leadership.

Thanks,

Max

Mac:

When I first came into your office, I was terrified. But you accepted me for me. You really made a difference, you made me feel like a real person again.

Thank you so very much for being the kind person you are and for going out of your way to help me. You will always be very special to me.

It was so nice of you!

Your loyal friend
forever

Brenda

Date: 03/05/98
From: Francis X. McDonnell
To: Staff, Coworkers and Friends
Subject: RETIREMENT

General Douglas McArthur address to Congress

OLD SOLDIERS NEVER DIE
THEY JUST FADE AWAY

The Old Soldier is retiring effective 03-06-98 from his position of Regional Director, Region #8. This will complete 52 happy years of service.

This will make Isobel very happy and allow us to visit our grandchildren, vacation, especially a trip to the "Old Sod" to visit the homestead.

It has been a great trip and now I plan to smell (not the roses) the jellies, chili, jams, salsa, muffins, etc.

Sincerely,
Francis X. McDonnell
Combat Medic WW II

Some of the Job Center Gang

Former Employees Who Made It!

Austin Burke
Scranton Area Chamber of Commerce President

Tim Speicher
T/R Associates, computer manufacturer in Archbald

Bob Davis and Ann Marie Novobilski
Manager, Scranton Job Center

TRAVELS WITH MAC & ISOBEL
(and most with Father Mark)

HERE are some of our destinations around the country and around the world:

- Paris (twice)
- London
- Ireland (three times)
- Riverboat cruises on the Mississippi and the Danube
- Panama Canal (twice)
- Switzerland (four times)
- Scotland
- Florida (six or seven times)
- Boston
- Nags Head (a cottage for seven years)
- Vienna
- Bratislava
- Budapest
- Novisad
- Belgrade

- Bucharest
- Lexington, Kentucky
- Seventeen-day cruise on the Queen Elizabeth II (her first cruise)
- Cruise to St. Thomas
- Norway
- Lady of Knock shrine in Ireland
- Alaska (four times)

- To Alaska, 9-15-11 -

On our last trip to Alaska, John Madden and I were to be in charge of two groups, 46 people total. When we landed in Seattle we were scheduled to take a bus into Canada, where we'd meet the cruise ship. I counted our group and came up with 44! After searching everywhere I still couldn't find the two missing people. When I called John in desperation he replied, "I forgot to tell you. Two little old ladies cancelled."

- Skidoo -

When I was in World War II, my aunt gave me the address of my uncle Skidoo, John McDonnell, who lived in Ireland. She wanted me to write to him, so I used to communicate with him during that period of time. On one occasion I sent him a picture of myself in my uniform.

I had become a combat medic and a staff sergeant, and my captain wanted me to enlist for another year. He knew my relationship to my uncle—grand-uncle it would've been —so he'd offered me a thirty day furlough in Ireland. I declined because I was more inclined to get home. I arrived home on Christmas Eve of 1945.

Many years later after my mom died, all the kids were given papers that pertained to them, including the pictures and letters I had given to my uncle Skidoo that he had returned to me. I used to always talk about Uncle Skidoo, so, thanks to my daughter Ellen, we made a trip to Ireland with my son-in-law to visit him. But he had died the year before. When we walked into his old house, his niece was there. And when I identified myself, she went over to the cabinet, took out my picture, and said, "Uncle John used to tell

me, '*Hold on to this picture, this man will return someday.*'"
Probably one of the most moving moments of my life.

We went back to Ireland several times and visited the estate. The estate consisted of an old shack with a tin roof at that point in time.

My relatives were glad to see us. They're only second and third cousins but they were very grateful. And later on we found out that some of our relatives lived in New Jersey and they came to visit us and we visited them so it was great. It was a great experience and we learned a lot. When I went back with my grandchildren and children, they were surprised to see where I had come from.

Some Irish traditions have been passed down in my family. Good cooking, eating, having a good time. A sense of humor. Recently a doctor told me I was born with *happy genes.*

This is the picture I sent to Skidoo. His niece returned it to me after his death.

- A Mac Story -

I asked Jay Sossa of Northeast Transportation in Clifford what it would cost to rent a bus to West Point for a football game. "Just pay the driver," he said. The bus was filled with staff from the Carbondale Job Center and their friends, as well as my friends.

The trip was run for several years, but the final trip was when the bus got stuck after we crossed the bridge into New York State. We pulled over and had a picnic, then Bruce Bloxham suggested that we try to start the bus by giving it a push. We loaded the beer, soda and sandwiches, as well as the girls, on the bus and pushed it about twenty feet. No luck, no start. So Sam Cerra bummed a ride to the nearest town.

We found a garage and were informed that all of the mechanics were off on Saturdays. BUT the garage owner had an owner that drove a school bus.... We loaded everyone and everything on board the school bus and got to West Point just in time for the kickoff (West Point lost). It was a great experience and it's great to tell the story, especially the part about pushing the bus!

- A Mac Story -

My son-in-law worked for ABC news, and he gave me a blue
ABC jacket. I had a lot of fun with it. People would see me
and they didn't know--they thought I worked for ABC!

We were in Ireland about 25 years ago. We went into this
little coffee shop, and there were a bunch of women there,
and they asked, "Do you really work for ABC?" "Oh, yeah,"
I said. "I travel the world! If you want to, we'll take your picture and maybe we'll use it on the news when we get back!"
So they go bananas. I chatted with them, and one said, "I
forgot to ask your name." "I'm Howard Cosell!" And one
lady said, "You look so different in your little box!"

With Father Mark in Switzerland

On the Queen Elizabeth II

Ireland

Alaska Cruise

Jelly factory in the cellar

Jam

The Sunday Times

May 30, 2001

Francis X. McDonnell makes jam, jelly, salsa and pesto. He donates jellies and jams for raffle baskets at the Jessup Triboro Church, the Interboro Library and his granddaughter's school in Maryland. Mac has a "client list" for his jams and jellies that includes National Public Radio news broadcasting personalities Nina Totenberg and Cokie Roberts. He always carries a jar or two with him in his car. "I never know who I'm going to give it to."

Although and outsider might say jelly and jam making is Mac's hobby, he sees it a little differently: "If I had to describe my hobby, it'd be people."

- Sweet Letters to Mac -

December 27, 1994

Thank you for the wonderful gift of fruitcake jam. It is my great pleasure to be your surgeon.

Eric Blomain, MD

October 27, 2009

Thanks for the great salsas and jams. We really appreciate things like that here in Japan.... Thanks again for the great treats, but especially for the support. Over here we say "Ichi Dan"--One Team!

With appreciation,

Three-star General Frank Wiencinski, Hawaii, Commander of Pacific Unit 45013

June 6

The jams are wonderful—and the basket is so attractive. Thanks so much for a special jar and a nice reminder of the McDonnell family we'll enjoy for months to come.

All the best,

Cokie Roberts

Christmas, 2010

I had toast and strawberry jam for breakfast and it was great. Thanks for remembering me—I'll remember the jars!

Warmest regards,

Judge James M. Munley

August 16, 2009

You're all so thoughtful and ever so kind! Over 1000 jars per year! That's an amazing array of your handsome portrait all over the country!

Thanks for keeping even the Bronx a bit sweeter!

January 1, 2010

You certainly know how to keep everybody in a jam! Thanks as always for your kindness!

January 10, 2011

Thanks to you, I'm all "jammed up" for the New Year!

January 15, 2012

Ninety years young and you're still outdoing Smuckers in ultimate taste and creativity!

Blessings and thanks.

March 23, 2012

My cup(board) overfloweth with your special treats! It will take me years to use up your thoughtful gifts! Hope you'll share your bounty with others! Again, thanks!

Msgr. Quinn

Dear Mac,

Thank you very much for donating the Super Large Basket of Mac's Homemade Jams and Jellies. It is always a big hit. We appreciate also that you personally sold so many tickets.

The success of the Festival is the result of the hard work, generosity and commitment of many like yourself who love St. Joseph's Center.

Thanks for your help,

Sister Maryalice

Happy New Year!

I was the lucky winner in the NPR holiday drawing of your wonderful homemade assortment. I also happen to work for one of the shows Ellen oversees. She is great to work for and a lot of fun. You have a true talent—and our toast and oatmeal has new life!

Thank you!

Renita

Head of Communication
British Embassy
Washington

5 January 2010

Dear Francis,

Thank you kindly for the card, and especially for the jams, which I have shared with colleagues here.

Thanks too for sharing your photograph of Marlborough Forest in 1944. The efforts of US and UK servicemen and women in World War Two remain extraordinary more than half a century later, and that experience of shared sacrifice remains the crucible in which the special relationship between our two countries was really forged.

With all very best wishes, and thanks once more,

Martin Longden

May 7, 2012

Dear Mr. McDonnell,

Your wonderful jams arrived just in time for my Passover dinner. We had the mint jelly with the lamb and one raspberry as a sauce for dessert. It was perfect! And now we are enjoying the others. Thank you so much.

I'm glad you enjoyed your trip to my hometown.

Cheers,

Cokie

(Cokie Roberts, of ABC News)

COUNTRY AND COMMUNITY

A Life Touched by Mac

Carmello Riotta left Sicily for the United States in 1968. Although he wasn't a citizen, he was drafted to serve in the U.S. Army and honorably discharged. On January 27, 1975, without a job, married to a Carbondale girl, he came to the Bureau of Employment Security office. The problem— although a veteran, as an alien, he couldn't be hired by the Tobyhanna Army Depot. Manager Francis McDonnell hired him as a Temporary Unemployment Claims interviewer while a member of Mac's staff, Tim Speicher, helped untangle a frustrating web of red tape. After numerous calls and letters to politicians, judges and bureaucrats, Tim succeeded. On April 7, 1975, Carmello Riotta began working at Tobyhanna—a veteran, and a citizen.

Throughout the United States, state employment service offices have a federal mandate to give preference to veterans. The difference in Carbondale, says Mr. McDonnell, is: "We stick to it and implement it."

"Every day is Veterans' Day in Carbondale," Mr. McDonnell smiles. He seems to be thinking—one old comrade to another—"You may not find a job here, but you'll certainly find a friend."   (*The Scranton Times*)

January 1, 2012

Thank you for your service and for all that you have done for our country. You seem like man that is full of energy and still very active! The homemade southwest salsa was delicious—my soldiers and I really enjoyed it.

I'm originally from Puerto Rico but moved to Wilkes-Barre when I was 13. I'm a graduate of Bloomsburg University and I received my commission from the ROTC program on campus in 2007. I have been to Kuwait, Qatar, Iraq and now Kosovo in my eleven years in the military.

I truly appreciate you and every other American that supports the troops and takes time and money out of their lives to make ours a little better. Thanks for praying for all of us over here, and God bless!

CPT Juan Fernandez
TFF-PCP KFR 15
APO AE 09340

Valley Advantage, January 20, 2012

Francis X. McDonnell recently celebrated his 90th birthday at Genetti Manor in Dickson City, with more than 80 friends and family. In lieu of gifts, guests were asked to make a contribution to the care and rehabilitation of Spc. Nicholas Staback, who was severely injured in Afghanistan. Through the generosity of these guests, a check for $3000 was presented to state Rep. Ed Staback, Nicholas's grandfather. Nicholas is currently being treated at Walter Reed Hospital, Maryland.

Frank, there are not enough words to tell you how touched we are for your overwhelming donation to Nicholas. It is special people like yourself that give Nicholas the strength to get up every day and face the challenges of his day.

His road of recovery will be long, but he is earning to walk again which is so amazing to see!

Once again from our entire family we thank you and want you to know we will never forget your kindness.

Eddie, Maria, Nicholas and Ryan Staback

Certificate of Nomination

Frances McDonnell

is hereby nominated by the
International Fellowship of Christians and Jews
As a follower in the path of the
Righteous gentiles
Who bravely stood in support and solidarity
with the biblical land of Israel and her people.

Rabbi Yechiel Eckstein

March 17, 2010

Dear Francis X,

On behalf of our library community, I would like to thank you for your unselfish devotion and tireless efforts exhibited in the performance of your duties as library trustee. I would also like to thank you for your hard work in making the conception of the Gino Merli Room possible. We declare you a Board member Emeritus.

Joan Guari, President
Valley Community Library Board

September 13, 1996

Please accept our most sincere thank-you for your part in the Scranton-Lackawanna Human Development Agency project to purchase winter coats for our Head Start Program youngsters. From all of us here, and of course the 700 youngsters—thanks again.

Fred Lettieri, Executive Director

Note from Mac: I have been a member of this committee since 1991. In 2011 we purchased 1430 coats.

From: Clem Goldberger, National World War II Museum

To: Roberts, Cokie B.

Sent: Tuesday, January 24, 2012

Dear Cokie,

Regarding Ms. Ellen McDonnell's father—it would be an honor and pleasure to set up a special visit. I know our President Dr. Nick Mueller will want to greet them personally, as will I.

Veteran's Day, 2004

Dear Mr. McDonnell,

There are not enough words to thank you for all of your time and effort in making the Gino Merli Room a reality. You made this sometimes-difficult process so much easier for me, and I truly appreciated your patience and kindness as I sorted through the many items for display. It is such a wonderful feeling of peace to see my late husband's memorabilia in such a beautiful setting in our hometown of Peckville. Although Gino was such a humble man and would have said that all this fuss was not necessary, he would be so proud to have this room be a special inspiration to the community and, most especially, its young people.

Your efforts in fundraising, planning, and developing the program for the dedication are greatly appreciated. I can only imagine all of the hours you spent to make everything so perfect.

On behalf of my children, Gino's sister and brother, and all of our family, I thank you from the bottom of my heart. We will be forever grateful. God bless you.

Mrs. Mary Merli and family

Mac and PFC Gino Merli

The Valley Community Library's Gino Merli Room was dedicated on September 16, 2004, in Peckville, PA.

My daughter Ellen keeps a close eye on Gino's mausoleum in Clifford to make sure there's always a fresh flag. Ike Refice, WWII veteran with a *Silver Star*, supplies us with the flags.

105

CHAPEL of the FOUR CHAPLAINS

The Chapel of the Four Chaplains is a national, not-for-profit organization founded in 1947, which recognizes and encourages observation of the unity which binds together Americans of all faiths. Patriotic in its nature, the Chapel celebrates the characteristic generosity, devotion to Gd and country, and love of all people which we share in common, It memorializes the courageous act of four Army Chaplains who gave their lifejackets to others when the troopship Dorchester was torpedoed on February 3, 1943, and hoors the 672 men who perished. The Chapel of the Four Chaplains is located in Building 649, the Chapel at the Philadelphia Naval Yard.

Francis X. McDonnell is Trustee, and has recommended many area men and women for recognition by the Chapel. A special program is held annually at Genetti's in Dickson City.

I have been fortunate to receive many awards from many organizations throughout the years. I started my program of seeking award recognition for deserving people in the area in 1956, launching it with a motion at a meeting of the Ambrose Revels Post 328 to honor a local boy, Dave Berger, who had made it in Philadelphia. I was Commander of the Post, and as a result over 350 local citizens responded and attended the program at the St. Thomas Aquinas church basement.

This was the start of over one hundred programs, which will continue through October, 2012 with awards to members of the local clergy.

Here are some of the local, county, state, and national awards I have secured for men and women who have lived a life of service:

American Legion/VFW awards

Awards for religious leaders

Chapel of the Four Chaplains

Kentucky Colonels

Tennessee Squires

State Physican of the Year (Dr. Michael Aronica, Dr. Thomas Coleman, Dr. Philip Henstell)

National Employer of the Year (Gentex Corp., Weston Corp., Monarch Pallet, Northeast Training Institute)

National Handicapped Employee (Bill Rinaldi)

Proceeds from the sale of
The Life of Mac will be donated to
the Valley Community Library in
Peckville, PA, and
the National World War II Museum
in New Orleans.

Additional copies may be purchased from
Mr. McDonnell. Call 570-876-5817 for information.

For information on publishing with Avventura Press, please email
lee@avventurapress.com

CPSIA information can be obtained at www.ICGtesting.com
Printed in the USA
BVOW070620161012

303066BV00001B/12/P